On the Job

Vet

Comparing Groups

Linda Claire

Vets help animals.

They help animals
stay healthy.

2 vets help 1 dog.

Woof!

1 vet helps 3 cats.

Meow, meow,
meow!

2 vets help
3 guinea pigs.

Squeak, squeak, squeak!

2 vets help
4 horses.

Neigh, neigh,
neigh, neigh!

1 vet helps
9 snakes.

Hiss, hiss, hiss,
hiss, hiss, hiss,
hiss, hiss, hiss!

1 vet helps 7 birds.

Chirp, chirp, chirp, chirp, chirp, chirp, chirp!

Problem Solving

Help the vet count the animals. Write how many there are. Compare the numbers using the sentences.

 ___

 ___

 ___

 ___

 ___

 ___

1. ___ is greater than ___.

2. ___ is less than ___.

3. ___ is equal to ___.

Answer Key

: 5; : 3; : 5;
: 4; : 1; : 7

1. Example: 7 is greater than 4.
2. Example: 1 is less than 3.
3. 5 is equal to 5.

Consultants

Nicole Belasco, M.Ed.
Kindergarten Teacher, Colonial School District

Colleen Pollitt, M.A.Ed.
Math Support Teacher, Howard County Public Schools

Publishing Credits

Rachelle Cracchiolo, M.S.Ed., *Publisher*
Conni Medina, M.A.Ed., *Managing Editor*
Dona Herweck Rice, *Series Developer*
Emily R. Smith, M.A.Ed., *Series Developer*
Diana Kenney, M.A.Ed., NBCT, *Content Director*
June Kikuchi, *Content Director*
Véronique Bos, *Creative Director*
Robin Erickson, *Art Director*
Stacy Monsman, M.A., and Karen Malaska, M.Ed., *Editors*
Michelle Jovin, M.A., *Associate Editor*
Fabiola Sepulveda, *Graphic Designer*

Image Credits: All images from iStock and/or Shutterstock.

Library of Congress Cataloging-in-Publication Data

Names: Claire, Linda, author.
Title: On the job : vet / Linda Claire.
Other titles: Vet
Description: Huntington Beach, CA : Teacher Created Materials, [2019] | Audience: K to grade 3.
Identifiers: LCCN 2017059686 (print) | LCCN 2018005967 (ebook) | ISBN 9781480759534 (e-book) | ISBN 9781425856151 (pbk.)
Subjects: LCSH: Veterinarians--Juvenile literature. | Animals--Juvenile literature.
Classification: LCC SF756 (ebook) | LCC SF756 .C53 2019 (print) | DDC 636.089092--dc23
LC record available at https://lccn.loc.gov/2017059686

Teacher Created Materials
5301 Oceanus Drive
Huntington Beach, CA 92649-1030
www.tcmpub.com

ISBN 978-1-4258-5615-1

Printed by: 51497
Printed in: China